T0283191

THE BASICS OF

RELIABILITY

THE BASICS OF

RELIABILITY

RONALD BLANK

PRODUCTIVITY
productivity press

NEW YORK, NEW YORK

Most Productivity Press books are available at quantity discounts when purchased in bulk. For more information contact our Customer Service Department (888-319-5852). Address all other inquiries to:

Productivity Press
444 Park Avenue South, Suite 604
New York, NY 10016
United States of America
Telephone: 212-686-5900
Fax: 212-686-5411
E-mail: info@productivitypress.com

Printed and bound by Malloy Lithographing, Inc.
in the United States of America

Library of Congress Cataloging-in-Publication Data

Blank, Ronald
    The basics of reliability / By Ronald Blank
        p. cm.
    ISBN 1-56327-302-0 (alk. paper)
    1. Reliability (Engineering) 2. Reliability. I Title

    TS173.B53 2004
    620'.00452—22

                                                    2004005234

07 06 05 04 10 9 8 7 6 5 4 3 2 1

Contents

CHAPTER 1

What Is Reliability?

DEFINITION AND PURPOSE OF RELIABILITY

When you feel that you can rely on something, the reason is that it always meets your expectations. It does what you want it to, when you want is to, and in the way you expect. That's why you rely on it.

The engineering definition of reliability is essentially the same, but is stated in language that is more technical. *The reliability of a process, product, or system is the probability that it will perform as specified, under the specified conditions, for the specified period of time.*

A high reliability is simply a high probability that this is so. Reliability engineers and customers may avoid the terms *high* or *low* when discussing reliability because they are relative. Reliability is either acceptable (as specified or contracted) or it is not.

Sometimes it is desirable to know the reliability of a product, usually a piece of hardware. Other times it is not the product reliability that is in question, but the reliability of the *process* that produced the product. Product reliability is important to the customer using the product, but process reliability is very important to the producer making the product. Any manufacturing process that does not work as specified is costly in terms of both downtime and scrap production, so manufacturers may test process reliability and improve it as necessary to minimize downtime and scrap production.

The specified *product* reliability of a manufactured product concerns how long or how often the product performs a specified function; for example, how many times the gun shoots before it jams, or how long a clothes washing machine will last before it needs repair. *Process* reliability concerns how long the process runs or how many process cycles are completed before the output of the process is *not* as specified. For example, the reliability of an automated packaging process refers to how long it will operate before something is mispackaged. For nonmanufacturing situations, reliability may focus on how often the goal of a procedure is realized as specified; for example, the procedure by which luggage is boarded on a commercial aircraft. If you define a procedure failure as placement of the luggage onto the wrong plane, then the reliability of the procedure concerns the probability that it will be on the correct airplane.

The specified conditions are often environmental, but they can also encompass energy levels, speeds, personnel, or any combination thereof. The specified time may be actual time measurements like hours, days, years, and so on, or it may be a specified number of *operation cycles*, or even the single use of a disposable item.

In any case, reliability is a *prediction* of the *probability of success*, based upon available data and resulting from observations and tests. Reliability testing and observations produce a probability that is expressed as a percent. However, that number is only a prediction.

A reliability prediction may be made for any of several purposes. It may help determine the feasibility of a new design or manufacturing process, so that a decision can be made as to whether or not to pursue it. The reliability prediction may also compare two or more products, processes, or systems to determine which one will last the longest or have the highest success. Often reliability qualifies a new vendor or manufacturing process. A reliability prediction may even be a selling point that induces a customer to choose your product over a competitor's.

How good a prediction is this? That is a matter of confidence. The higher the confidence number the better the prediction. Validity of the reliability calculation depends on the validity of the data used to calculate it, and the *confidence level* of the sample. That data validity is primarily a matter of test validity. The confidence level of the sample is statistically determined.

While specific components like a steel bolt or an electronic transistor have their own reliability, more typically, reliability needs to be determined for complex machines. Such reliabilities are actually composite reliabilities of the individual components.

Processes such as manufacturing a product are made up of process components. Each operation of a manufacturing process is a component of the process, and each operation may be comprised of individual steps. Each of these has its own reliability, so the overall process reliability is actually a composite reliability as well.

Reliability can also be the probability of successfully completing a mission. Think of the space shuttle bringing a satellite into space and returning. This is a process involving the interaction of all the applicable hardware, software, people, and procedures necessary to complete the space shuttle mission. Each of these is a component of the mission completion system and each has its own component reliability. Together they determine the mission reliability, that is, the probability that the space shuttle will successfully put the satellite into the correct orbit and return safely.

To summarize, reliability is a prediction of the probability that something will perform as specified, under the specified conditions, for the specified period of time. The reliability prediction is usually expressed as a percent. The prediction is made from observations and data resulting from reliability testing and known *failure rate* data. The principles of reliability apply to manufactured items, processes, procedures, people, and systems alone, or in any combination. The validity of the prediction depends on the validity of the data used in the reliability calculation and requires valid testing with proper sampling.

BENEFITS OF RELIABILITY

The reliability calculation is useful to both the supplier and the customer. To the customer it tells the risk undertaken when he or she buys and uses the product. Highly complex products, or products to be used in harsh environments, are a greater usage risk to the user. Extremely expensive products represent a greater financial risk. Thus, the reliability prediction helps determine if the risk is worth taking. There may also be safety or liability concerns if product failure results in danger or death.

Suppliers benefit from reliability calculations in several ways. Reliability can be the standard by which they benchmark and compare their product to that of the competition, or even be a selling point to enhance the product's attractiveness to customers. Since manufacturing process failures result in downtime, the reliability prediction of the manufacturing process is actually a means for predicting process downtime.

Reliability can even be applied to people, that is, the probability that a person (or group) will successfully perform the specified task, under the specified conditions, for the specified period of time. This can identify training needs, manpower requirements, and procedure or system flaws.

Determining reliability requires an understanding of the basic concepts, proper sampling, valid testing, measuring of successes and failures, and some mathematical calculations, all of which are discussed in the following chapters of this book

CHAPTER 2
Basic Concepts

Reliability requires the understanding of certain concepts and how to apply them. In this chapter the reader will explore some of the most important and useful ones. This chapter is not intended to be an exhaustive glossary of reliability terms, but rather an introduction to the most common concepts as applied to reliability. Further discussion of some of these topics will be presented in more detail in the chapters ahead.

Probability of success is the probability, expressed as a percent, that a thing or process will meet the specification for which reliability is being examined. Notice that success always relates to a specification. The question is not whether or not it works, but whether it works *as specified*. This is similar to the concept of success as applied to sampling. Sampling success occurs when the inspection trial uncovers what the examiner (inspector or tester) is looking for. Probability of success is essentially the same thing as the reliability, but the term *probability of success* is used primarily for single-use or unique items, and system missions.

Operating life is the length of time, or number of operations, the item or process under examination will continue to be acceptable to the specification before it fails to meet the specification. For a nonrepairable item, it is essentially the same as *Time to failure.* An example might be the number of hours a computer disk drive operates before it fails. Operating life can apply to processes, products, or systems.

In the case of a repairable item, operating life may be the time at which the repairs are no longer economical, or a specific predefined *failure mode* occurs.

Operating life always relates to a performance specification and a set of environmental conditions, since a change in the conditions can affect how long something lasts. Life tests are sometimes accelerated by altering the environment. Frequently ambient temperature or pressure is modified to accelerate the life test. One must be careful with *accelerated life tests* because they can produce erroneous conclusions if the manner in which the environment accelerates time to failure is not proved or is misunderstood.

Failure rate (FR), is the number of reliability test samples that fail at a specified time. It is expressed as failures per device hour. *Device-hours* are the sample size multiplied by either test time or number of operations. For example, a sample of 1,000 transistors is in operation for 1,000 hours. Thus, 1,000 transistors operating for 1,000 hours each is 1,000,000 *device operation hours*, because 1,000 X 1,000 = 1,000,000. If seven of them fail, that is seven failures out of one million device operation hours, or a failure rate of seven parts per million. Of course, for this reliability test to be valid, the transistors would all have to be subject to identical test parameters of power, temperature, test circuit, and so on. Failure rate is usually reported as the maximum percent of failures per 1,000 device-hours or operations, and sometimes as parts per million. FR is equivalent to the probability of failure.

Time to failure is the time elapsed from the onset of the function (or mission start) to the failure of the device or process (or mission failure). In reporting time to failure, it must be specified whether the time to failure is the time to the first failure, the time to a specified number of sample failures, time to a specific failure mode, or the average (mean) time to failure.

When applied to nonrepairable items, time to failure is the basic measure of reliability and is usually expressed in terms of the average time to failure known as the **mean time to failure** (MTF or MTTF). If done with a sample, it may be reported as the sample MTF.

Mean time between failures (MTBF), is also very commonly used in reliability studies. It means the time elapsed or number of operations between successive failures of the same *repairable* device. It may be the time between occurrences of the same failure mode, or, if so specified, a group of different failure modes. One example concerns an automobile. If the brakes need to be repaired an average of every 40,000 miles, then 40,000 miles is the MTBF for the brake system of the car. This is a *single failure mode* MTBF. But if the car needs brakes at 30,000 miles, and new transmission at 50,000, and has a radiator leak at 90,000 miles, then you can specify that the MTBF calculation be based on all three failure modes. In the case of our car, there is failure at 30,000 miles, then another failure 20,000 miles later (the transmission), and a radiator problem 40,000 miles later (at 90,000). The *multiple failure mode* MTBF is the average of 30,000, 20,000, and 40,000, which calculates to an average multiple failure mode MTBF of 30,000 miles.

20,000
30,000
+ 40,000
90,000

then divide by 3 to get the average

90,000 / 3 = 30,000

so the multiple failure modes MTBF is 30,000

Before beginning the reliability test, you must determine which type of MTBF you are interested in, single or multiple, and when reporting the MTBF, you must specify which one it is.

Failure mode is the reason why something failed to meet the operating specification. In the case of a single component, it tells what happened to the component that caused it to fail. In the case of a subassembly, or a more complex machine, it can be a detailed report or simply the identification of which component failed, with a brief statement of what happened to the component that resulted in failure. The degree of detail in failure mode reporting varies slightly from one company to the next. It varies far more between different industries. The aircraft, automotive, and nuclear power industries typically use detailed failure-mode reporting.

Often the reporting of a failure mode refers to a **Failure mode and effects analysis** (FMEA). Briefly, this is a listing of what can go wrong with a process or product and the effects of the failure. FMEAs are usually done before the product goes into production. Each failure mode is rated for probability of occurrence, severity of failure, and effect on customer (or probability the customer will notice the failure).

These ratings are then used to calculate a **risk priority number** (RPN). Preventive action is then applied to failure modes having RPNs above a specified threshold. Reliability testing often provides valuable insight on the failure modes and gives realistic data to determine the ratings. The implementation of preventive actions called for on a FMEA can be a major contribution toward reducing scrap and downtime. Extensive literature exists on FMEAs.

Test validity is the most often debated issue of reliability. A valid test must either realistically simulate actual usage conditions or have a *known and proved correlation* to actual usage. The closer the test conditions are to actual usage conditions, the more valid the test is. Reliability test results may be biased by insufficient realism, and sometimes they are. The test must be carried out in such a manner as to eliminate any influence that could affect the outcome. It must therefore be objective. Some companies prohibit both equipment and personnel from having any relationship to the manufacturer. Yet it is worthwhile for the manufacturers to perform their own reliability testing, if it is done fairly and objectively. It is especially useful to determine the reliability of a process or product prior to going to market.

Other concepts related to reliability are availability, maintainability, and capability. Each has it own definition in relation to reliability. **Availability** is the percent of time a product or process is ready for use without expenditure of additional effort or unplanned waiting. "Ready for use," is a relative term, and should be well specified. **Maintainability** is often measured by **Mean Time To Repair (MTTR)**. It results from a planned maintainability program. **Mean cost to repair** (MCR) is another measure of maintainability. It is used when the decision of whether or not to repair something is based on economics. If the average cost of repair exceeds a predefined threshold, the item is not considered repairable. **Capability** is a comparison of the actual product or process performance to a specification. Readers familiar with *statistical process control* (SPC) are already familiar with process capability. A product capability is similarly a ratio of the specified performance of a product to its actual performance.

The glossary provides meanings of other reliability terms. It contains all terms specific to reliability that are within the scope of this book.

CHAPTER 3
Sampling

CHOOSING A SAMPLING PLAN

The choice of sampling plans in reliability testing depends on several considerations — the purpose of the test, the underlying *frequency distribution* of the characteristic being checked, the available resources, and sample *availability.* Also considered are cost, time, and the desired confidence level.

A *sample* for a *feasibility* study needs only to be large enough to confirm the possibility of manufacture, along with the repeatability and reproducibility of the manufacturing process. Reliability testing to determine if the reliability of a manufacturing lot meets specifications requires a larger sampling based on lot size and desired quality levels. Such sampling plans resemble those found in ANSI/ASQ Z1.4, which is a commonly used plan for sampling by attributes. Reliability testing to determine the reliability of a design or product, when it is unknown, usually requires sampling per an *exponential sampling plan*, as, for example, during product development.

FEASIBILITY STUDY SAMPLING

Sometimes reliability testing is done at the very beginning of the research and development phase, when the designer is still trying to determine the practicality of producing the product at all. Normally this is part of a feasibility study.

During a feasibility study, the designing activity really wants to know three things:

1. Is it possible to manufacture the product so that it functions as specified under the specified conditions for the specified period of time?
2. If it is possible, can the manufacturing process be repeated?
3. If it can be repeated, is the manufacturing process reproducible?

There is a difference between *repeatability* and *reproducibility*. A process is *repeatable* when the same person (or department, work team, etc.) can successfully make the part more than once using the same equipment (machines, set of tools, etc.). A process is *reproducible* if it can be successfully done with more than one set of equipment, and the second set of equipment and tools can reproduce the results of the first set. Alternatively, a process is reproducible when more than one person (or group of people) can reproduce the results obtained by the first person (or group) performing the process. All manufacturing processes must be both repeatable and reproducible unless they are intended to manufacture a unique item.

Nonstatistical sampling is usually used for these feasibility studies. Making one of something such that it meets all requirements proves it is indeed possible to make. Manufacturing two of something proves that the manufacturing process can be repeated. Manufacturing two with one set of equipment, or people, and then manufacturing two more with a second set, proves that the process is reproducible. Thus, for a feasibility study a minimum sample of four is needed. Additional samples in the repeatability and reproducibility activities add to confidence. Some companies use five in each set for a total sample of ten pieces.

SAMPLING TO VERIFY RELIABILITY

Not all reliability testing is performed so early in product development, nor is it necessarily for the purpose of determining feasibility. Reliability testing is sometimes done at receiving inspection to verify that the commodity received does in fact have the reliability it is supposed to have. Verifying reliability at incoming inspection is sometimes done for certain failure modes on critical components where failure would have catastrophic results, but more often it is done only on the first shipment received in order to qualify a product, process, or vendor.

Reliability testing may also be done before shipment, as an audit of outgoing product reliability. Both are cases of reliability verification rather than initial reliability determination.

In either case, sample size is best determined statistically. Do not make the mistake of using a constant percentage of lot size as a sample size, for example, always taking a 5% or 10% sample. Although constant percentage sampling may seem logical, it is always unwise. The number of samples taken on small lots may be too small to give adequate confidence and the number of samples from large lots may be too large and therefore wasteful and inefficient. Also, the *sampling risks* are unknown and variable. Constant percentage sampling results in costly and inefficient reliability testing and can even lead to an incorrect conclusion.

If you wish to simply verify that not more than a specified percentage of a lot will fail for any reason under specified conditions, after a specified *minimum* time period, regardless of other reliability measures, then what you are performing is a simple pass/fail test. For that, all you need is a standard binomial distribution-based attribute sampling plan for lot-by-lot inspection such as ANSI/ASQ Z 1.4.

For example, suppose you are testing a sample of light bulbs to verify that they will last more than 100 hours, a specified percent of failures being allowed. Any given light bulb will either last a minimum of 100 hours or it won't. This is no different than dimensional inspection of a purchased part in that a measured dimension is either the proper size or it is not. Such sampling plans are typically attribute-type *average quality level* plans such as ANSI/ASQ Z1.4. Based on the now discontinued MIL-STD-105E, this sampling specification provides sampling tables for producers and consumers. The attribute sampling scheme used may be *single sampling, double sampling,* or *multiple sampling.* Single sample plans are the easiest to use but have the largest sample sizes. Multiple plans are more difficult to use but result in the fewest samples being used. Double sampling plans are a good balance between the two.

If you are the purchaser of a device and are qualifying a vendor, process, or product, select either a *lot tolerance percent defective* (LTPD) (also called *rejectable quality level,* RQL) plan or an AQL plan. Use LTPD plans for isolated or infrequent lots. Use AQL plans for a continuing series of lots.

With the LTPD equal to the maximum allowable failure percent, $Pa = 5$ plans will give you 95% confidence that the percent failure of the lot will not exceed the LTPD. $Pa = 10$ plans give 90% confidence. After determining the confidence level, choose a sampling plan that has the specified allowable defect rate.

If you are the manufacturer and are auditing reliability by checking the percent of a lot that will fail for any reason during the minimum test time, then select a sample where the AQL equals the maximum percent of failures you can allow. If the sampling plan accepts the lot, you can be confident that the rest of the lot will last the minimum time, with a failure rate averaging the same as the AQL *on a continuing series of lots*. Remember, AQLs are meant to apply to a series of lots produced under the same conditions. Your risk of rejecting a good sample is *alpha.* The probability of the lot being accepted when the defect rate exceeds the AQL is 1–alpha. You can determine the alpha risk level on the operations characteristics (OC) curve for the sample size and acceptance number you have chosen. Also on the OC curve is the probability of accepting the lot when the quality is at the RQL. This is called *beta.* Alpha plus beta is the total sampling risk. The sample confidence is 1 minus the total sampling risk. See Figure 3-1 for an illustration of OC curve use.

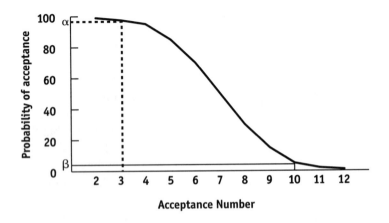

Graph shows at 3 defects probability of acceptance is 97.5%, so probability of rejections, α, is 2.5%. Probability of acceptance at 10 defects is only 5% so β ια 5%.

Figure 3-1. Operation Characteristics Curve Showing Sampling Risk

Remember that these attribute sampling plans are used in reliability to verify whether or not the device will function longer than a specified minimum time with a specified percent of functional failures. Such reliability testing is done only for minimum operating life *verification*, not for initial reliability determination.

SAMPLING TO DETERMINE RELIABILITY

Reliability tests are also done during the product development phase of the production cycle. In this case, the purpose is usually to determine what the actual reliability is and whether or not it meets the requirements. Most reliability testing is done to determine the actual reliability, often measured as FR, MTF/MTTF, or MTBF. A common purpose for reliability testing is to determine device failure rate (FR), which is often expressed in parts per thousand hours of operation, or parts per million operations. Testing performed for any of these purposes requires the proper selection of sampling plans. Which one you use depends on the underlying frequency distribution of the characteristic being tested. Figure 3-2 shows some typical distributions.

If you are testing to determine the FR or MTF of a physical property, such as shear strength or impact resistance of a uniform material under specified usage conditions, then, more often than not, the underlying distribution is normal, also called Gaussian. Any sampling plan based on the normal distribution can be used. Classic attribute sampling plans like ANSI/ASQ Z1.4 can also be used because the binomial distribution on which they are based is close enough to the normal distribution to pass most tests of normality.

Testing MTF due to metal fatigue, corrosion, or any time dependent failure mode usually requires sampling plans based on the exponential distribution, such as those found in military specifications or other reliability books. MTF of electronic components usually occurs randomly over time and so also has an exponential distribution. Furthermore, the exponential distribution always applies whenever there is a single failure mode if the failure events occur at random times, and the probability of the next failure is independent of the time of

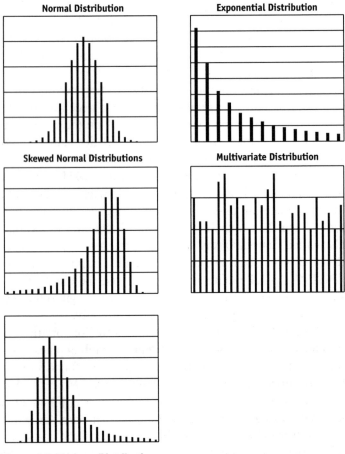

Figure 3-2. Various Distributions

the previous failure. In performing life tests to determine MTF or MTBF, the determination of sample size also depends on whether or not you will be sampling with or without replacement. In other words, will you remove, but keep track of, failed test samples and replace them with new ones during the test? Producer's risk (alpha), consumer's risk (beta), sample cost, and available test time are other factors to consider in determining the sample size. Still other factors are the specified mean life, the specified proportion of the lot that is allowed to fail before the whole lot is considered to be unacceptable, and the confidence ratio, which is related to alpha and beta. Table 3-1 is a sampling table for the exponential distribution of sampling without replacement, when alpha = .05 and beta = .10. Table 3-2 is for sampling with replacement. The sample size is selected from one of the multiples of the termination number (sample reject number) and is commonly 2r, 4r, 8r, 10r, or 20r (see Tables 3-1 and 3-2).

For example: you have received a shipment of staplers. You define a failure as the occasion when the staple gets jammed inside the stapler and it fails to staple. You want to verify the reliability of the lot. Find the sampling plan for sampling without replacement which has a 95% probability of accepting a lot having a specified mean life of 1,000 stapling operations. Assume your specification calls for a sampling plan where you accept the lot on 4 but reject on 5 failures, and you have 10 sample staplers available for testing.

The sampling scheme in Table 3-1 has a producer's risk of 5%, so it meets your 95% percent acceptance requirement. Your reject number (r) is 5. You have 10 sample staplers, so

TABLE 3-1. Sampling Without Replacement

Reject

Number	Sample Size as Multiples of r					
r	2r	3r	4r	5r	10r	20r
1	0.026	0.017	0.013	0.101	0.005	0.003
2	0.104	0.065	0.048	0.038	0.018	0.009
3	0.168	0.103	0.075	0.058	0.028	0.014
4	0.217	0.132	0.095	0.074	0.036	0.017
5	0.254	0.153	0.110	0.086	0.041	0.020
6	0.284	0.170	0.122	0.095	0.045	0.022
7	0.309	0.185	0.132	0.103	0.049	0.024
8	0.330	0.197	0.141	0.110	0.052	0.025
9	0.348	0.207	0.148	0.115	0.055	0.027
10	0.363	0.216	0.154	0.120	0.057	0.028
20	0.451	0.266	0.189	0.147	0.070	0.034
25	0.475	0.280	0.199	0.154	0.073	0.036
50	0.536	0.315	0.223	0.173	0.082	0.040
75	0.564	0.331	0.235	0.182	0.086	0.042
100	0.581	0.340	0.242	0.187	0.089	0.043

TABLE 3-2. Sampling With Replacement

Reject

Number	Sample Size as Multiples of r					
r	2r	3r	4r	5r	10r	20r
1	0.026	0.017	0.013	0.010	0.005	0.003
2	0.089	0.059	0.044	0.036	0.018	0.009
3	0.136	0.091	0.068	0.055	0.027	0.014
4	0.171	0.114	0.085	0.068	0.034	0.017
5	0.197	0.131	0.099	0.079	0.039	0.020
6	0.218	0.145	0.109	0.087	0.044	0.022
7	0.235	0.156	0.117	0.094	0.047	0.023
8	0.249	0.166	0.124	0.100	0.05	0.025
9	0.261	0.174	0.130	0.104	0.052	0.026
10	0.271	0.181	0.136	0.109	0.054	0.027
20	0.331	0.221	0.166	0.133	0.066	0.033
25	0.348	0.232	0.174	0.139	0.070	0.035
50	0.390	0.260	0.195	0.156	0.078	0.039
75	0.409	0.273	0.204	0.164	0.082	0.041
100	0.421	0.280	0.210	0.168	0.084	0.042

your sample is the 2r multiple of r. The row r = 5 intersects the column 2r at .254. Multiply the .254 times the specified 1,000 hours and you have a sample test plan of testing 10 staplers for 254 stapling operations each. The MTF does not meet the specification if 5 staplers jam before they complete 254 operations each.

SAMPLING COMPLEX DEVICES WITH MULTIPLE FAILURE MODES

Multiple failure causes and complex devices comprised of any combination of electrical, electronic, and mechanical parts, any of which can fail, usually have a *Weibull distribution.* This is actually a family of distributions capable of describing failure probabilities in almost any situation. The sampling plan to use depends on the shape of the Weibull distribution. If the failure frequency Weibull distribution shape is unknown, you must first determine it before choosing a sampling plan. There are two ways to do this.

If time and other resources allow, the surest way is to take a sample of 50 to 100 units and test them all to failure, recording the elapsed time period or number of operations before each device fails. Then plot the data as a *histogram.* The shape of the histogram is the shape of the distribution and determines which sample plan to use.

Due to time limitations, sample availability, and cost, testing so many samples all to failure may not be practical. The alternative is to take a sample of about ten pieces and test them all to failure. Then plot the results on Weibull graph paper. Determining the *shape parameter* from the Weibull graph will tell you the type of distribution. Refer to Figure 3-3 as you follow the procedure indicated below.

1. Graph the ten data points on the Weibull paper. Draw a line connecting the data points. Refer to this as the fitted line. If the line is curved, subtracting the same constant from each point will often result in a straight line plot.

2. Draw a straight line from the fitted line to the estimation point on the paper. This is usually in one corner of the paper. The shape parameter value is where this line crosses the shape scale.

If the Weibull plotting paper you have does not show an estimation point, the shape parameter is the slope of the fitted line. If you do not have Weibull plotting paper, then a functional estimation of the shape parameter can also be made by this equation:

Shape parameter = -3.076 - 20.99(S/X) + 9.516 $e^{(S/X)}$

where S = standard deviation of the data and X = the average of the data.

The shape parameter tells you the kind of distribution you have. If the shape parameter equals 1 or less, then the distribution is exponential and requires an exponential sampling plan. A shape parameter >1 and < 3.3 is a unimodal distribution, skewed high (to the right), with lower shape parameters indicating more skewness. Shape parameters >3.3 but < 3.8 indicate a more or less normal distribution, therefore ANSI/ASQ Z

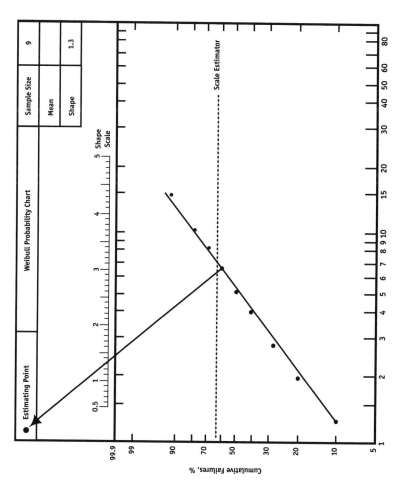

Figure 3-3. Weibull Probability Chart

1.4 can be used. Any shape parameter > 3.8 is a unimodal distribution, skewed low (left), with higher shape parameters indicating greater degrees of skewness and greater peakedness of the mode. The Weibull plotting paper tells what the distribution shape parameter is using a small sample. The distribution shape parameter tells you what sampling plan to use.

If Weibull probability paper is not available, or if it shows a skewed distribution neither normal nor exponential, or even if the sampling plans you have are all for normal distributions, the data can be normalized. *Normalization* of the data means manipulating all of the data mathematically so that the frequency distribution will have a normal curve, while the data still validly represents the population from which it came. After data is normalized, any sampling plan appropriate to a normal distribution can be used. One common normalization method is to apply the *central limit theorem*. Stated simply, the central limit theorem says that when a series of small sample groups is taken from the same population, the averages calculated from each of the sample groups will be normally distributed (not the data itself, but the averages). For example, if you take 20 samples of 10 pieces each, and calculate the average for each one of the 10-piece samples, you will have 20 averages and those averages themselves will be normally distributed. The averages are then used as if they are raw data. The closer the original data are to being normally distributed, the smaller those sample groups can be. Larger sample groups will show normality with fewer sample averages.

Two drawbacks to using the central limit theorem in reliability is that your calculations and conclusions must be on the averages, not on the raw data, and your sample size is not individuals units, but rather the number of smaller sample groups from which you calculated the averages. So if your sample plan calls for 20 samples, that is actually 20 samples of 10 pieces each, a total of 200 pieces. Moreover, sometimes the large number of measurements or samples necessary to calculate the required number of averages is not practical. In that case, you may wish to try *data transformation.*

Transformation is the second way to normalize data. This is simply the algebraic manipulation of the raw data by a single standardized function. You perform the transformation by applying the transforming equation to each data point individually so that you end up with a new set of data that is a transformation of the original data set. After such a transformation, if the transformed data is still not normal, then the central limit theorem must be applied if normality is to be obtained. Sometimes neither method can be applied, so the data cannot be normalized. In that case, sampling plans based on other sampling distributions are necessary. The most common transformations are shown in table 3-3.

The validity of any sample depends on the selection of the correct plan for the type of frequency distribution you have. That is why it is so important to determine the distribution shape. If the samples are drawn from a larger population, whether it is a pilot lot or production lot, the sample validity also depends on random drawing of the samples.

In any case, for the sample to be valid, the individual sample units must all be manufactured by the same process and should not be different in treatment, age, storage, or processing.

Table 3-3. Transformations for Normalizing Sample Data

Original Distribution Shape	Weibull Shape Parameter	Transformation
Unimodal, skewed high but slightly concave below mode	> 1 < 3	square root (X)
Unimodal, skewed high entirely convex	> 2 < 3.3	log e or log 10 (X)
Unimodal, skewed low	> 3.8 < 4.5	log (X / 1 − X) natural or base ten log
Unimodal, very skewed low	> 4.5	log ((1 + X) / (1 − X)) Fisher transformation

TRANSPOSING TIME AND QUANTITY IN SAMPLE PLANS

Another concept in reliability sampling is *time-quantity transposition.* If you are testing to determine failure rate, you can test either a small number of samples for a longer time, or a large number of samples for a shorter time, depending on your resources. The exponential sampling plans shown in Tables 3-1 and 3-2 do allow for transposition of time and quantity. The 4r is twice the sample of 2r and has significantly less test time.

Table 3-4 is a time-quantity transposition table that applies to all exponential distribution-based sample plans. It tells you the number of *device operation hours* or number of operations for specific test-time-to-expected-life ratios, at reject numbers up to ten failures. For example, assume a shipment of light bulbs is received and a mean life of 1,000

Table 3-4. Time-Quantity Transposition of Reliability Samples Based on the Exponential Distribution

Sample sizes are the minimum number of sample units to test to be 90% confident that the lot MTTF or MTBF is as specifed.

Acceptance Number	Ratio of availible test-time-to-expected-life								
	0.5	0.2	0.1	0.05	0.02	0.01	0.005	0.002	0.001
0	5	12	24	47	116	231	461	1152	2303
1	9	20	40	79	195	390	778	1946	3891
2	12	28	55	109	266	533	1065	2662	5323
3	15	35	69	137	333	668	1337	3341	6881
4	19	42	83	164	398	798	1599	3997	7994
5	22	49	97	190	462	927	1855	4638	9275
6	25	56	110	217	528	1054	2107	5267	10533
7	28	68	123	246	589	1178	2355	5886	11771
8	31	70	136	269	648	1300	2599	6498	12995
9	34	76	149	294	709	1421	2842	7103	14206
10	37	83	161	319	770	1541	3082	7704	15407

hours is specified, but only 50 hours are available for testing. Assume also that your sampling requires that you accept the shipment on 0 failures and reject it on 1. Therefore, 50 hours being available for a 1,000 hour expected mean life indicates a test-time-to-expected-life ratio of 50/1,000 or .05. Because the operating life of light bulbs follows the exponential distribution, Table 3-4 must be used. Entering Table 3-4 in the column for the .05 ratio and going down to the row for the desired reject/accept number of 0, we see that according to this sampling table, we must test 47 light bulbs for 50 hours. If there are no failures, the lot passes, and you can be 90% confident that the entire lot has a mean expected life of 1,000 hours. If you had more test time available, but fewer samples, you could transpose the time to something like 100 hours. This would be a test-time-to-expected-life ratio of .1. At an acceptance of 0 defects, that's a sample size of only 24 units. This transposition of time and quantity works for failure rates expressed as hours or number of operational repetitions *when failure is a random occurrence*.

Table 3-5 tells us the sample sizes for various test-time-to-life-expectancy ratios for attribute-type sample plans. For example, let's say we are verifying the reliability of a shipment of relays that are supposed to last a minimum of 1,000,000 operations. Our sample plan calls for 20 samples to be operated for 1,000,000 operations, but we have time for only 10,000 operations. That is a test-time-to-expected-life ratio of .01. Looking at Table 3-5, we go across the row for a

Table 3-5. Time-Quantity Transposition of Reliability Samples for Attribute Sampling Plans

Original Sample Size*	Ratio of availible test-time-to-life expectancy								
	0.5	0.2	0.1	0.05	0.02	0.01	0.005	0.002	0.001
3	6	15	30	60	150	300	600	1500	3000
5	10	25	50	100	250	500	1000	2500	5000
8	16	40	80	160	400	800	1600	4000	8000
13	26	65	130	260	650	1300	2500	6500	13000
20	40	100	200	400	1000	2000	4000	10000	20000
32	64	160	320	640	1600	3200	6400	16000	32000
50	100	250	500	1000	2500	5000	10000	25000	50000
80	160	400	800	1600	4000	8000	16000	40000	80000
125	250	625	1250	2500	6250	12500	25000	62500	125000
200	400	1000	2000	4000	10000	20000	40000	100000	200000

* Divide the the original sample accept/reject number for the sample size and AQL desired by the test-time-to-expectancy ratio to get new accept/reject number for transposed sample.

sample size of 20 until we come to the column for the ratio of .01. There we see that we will need a sample size of 2,000 to compress the test time down to only 10,000 operations.

SUMMARY OF RELIABILITY SAMPLING

Here is a summary of how reliability testing sample plans are determined.

1. If doing a feasibility test, use a minimum sample of four. Two for each part of the reproducibility testing. For added confidence, use more. For feasibility testing, there is no economically sound benefit for using more than a total of ten samples.

2. If verifying that a lot has the specified minimum life, use a standard attribute sample plan and stop the test when either the reject number has failed, or the minimum life has been reached, whichever comes first.

3. Use a sampling plan based on the exponential distribution whenever there is a single failure mode that occurs at random times and the probability of the next failure is independent of the time of the previous failure.

4. If the frequency distribution of the failures is unknown, use a Weibull plot to determine the distribution shape or, if practical, do a test sample of 50 to 100 units and plot the histogram to determine the distribution type.

5. Use data transformations or the central limit theorem to normalize data only as a last resort.

6. Once you know which sampling scheme to use, it will apply to that particular characteristic on the same parts all the time, so you need not determine it again for future reliability testing.

7. Limitations of test time or sample availability can be overcome by transposing test time and quantity.

CHAPTER 4

Measuring Reliability

SPECIFYING AND RECORDING RELIABILITY

All reliability measurements involve specified conditions and a specified function by which failure is defined. It is always necessary to specify both the function of the product or process, and the conditions in which the function is performed, to determine when a failure occurs. The specified conditions are most often environmental, but need not be. They can include the identity of the person who operates the process or product, and when, how often, and under what circumstances the product or process is operated. The circumstances can be any specified conditions.

Regardless of the purpose of the reliability testing, certain considerations should be specified and recorded for any reliability test. They are:

1. Environmental conditions during the test.
2. Any time-accelerating factors (if not covered in item 1).
3. Duration of test (usually specified in hours or number of operating cycles).

4. Number of sample units (or process runs) tested.
5. Operational parameters like speed, pressure, power input, etc.
6. Failure criteria.
7. Confidence level of the sample.
8. Purpose of the test.

During the reliability testing, the environmental conditions and operational parameters must be monitored and controlled to assure that throughout the testing they are as specified. The reliability test will be invalidated if they go out of specification at any time.

In addition to any contractual or quality system requirements concerning traceability of reliability test data, all reliability test data must be traceable to the exact lot from which the samples came. If there is more than one reliability test station, you may also want to have the test records indicate which reliability test station was used.

MEASURING PROCESS RELIABILITY

The reliability measurements of failure rate (FR), mean time to failure (MTF), and mean time between failures (MTBF) apply to both products and processes. The function of any process is to change the input into the output. The output needs to be specified not only to identify the output, but to determine the completion and the purpose of the process. In the case of a manufacturing process, completion would be the successful manufacture of a product. In the case of a service-type process, it would apply to the completion of whatever service the process provides. The transportation of freight, the settlement of an insurance claim, or the education of students, are all service processes that can have specified goals and conditions that define a failure. An aborted process is also a process failure. This occurs when a process fails to run to completion, either by stopping on its own or being stopped by an operator.

In testing the process, a process sample unit is one complete process cycle or one countable or measurable instance of completed output from the process. Examples of this are one insurance claim settled, one shipment of freight arriving at its destination, or one student educated. If a manufacturing process is being tested, then a process sample unit is one unit of product manufactured from one complete process cycle.

Once the purpose of the reliability testing is known, the sample plan determined, and the definition of failure is specified, then the test method is determined. For processes, this is simply a matter of performing the process as specified for the appropriate number of times required for the sample size.

Failure rate for the process is the number of times the goal of the process was not fulfilled in the specified manner when the process was run. It is often expressed as per mil (parts per thousand), calculated from the number of failures divided by the number of process runs, times 1,000.

Example: 3 shipments out of 50 failing to reach their destination is

$$(3/50) = .06$$
$$.06 \times 1000 = 60$$

so the FR is 60 parts per thousand

It may also be expressed as a percent. Simply multiply by 100 instead of 1,000. So 3 failures out of 50 is

3/50=.06

.06 X 100 = 6

or 6 out of 100, which is a 6% FR

MTF for a process is obtained by running the process and recording the time from initial process start-up to the first failure, and then starting the process again and recording time to the first failure again. Repeat this for the sample size number of times, and compute the average time from start-up to failure. This is the process of MTF.

Process MTBF is obtained by running the process continuously and recording the time between each successive failure and computing the average. You must specify whether the MTBF is being determined for single failure mode (the same failure mode repeating over and over again), a combination of failure modes, a specified failure mode that repeats, or any failure mode. For manufacturing processes that do not need to be shut down at each failure, MTBF may be a better measure of *process reliability* than MTF.

Since highly reliable processes are usually more cost efficient to run, it is prudent to take action to improve process reliability. If your process directly involves your customer, or is publicly visible, your reputation may be made or broken on process reliability alone.

MEASURING PRODUCT RELIABILITY

In testing *product reliability*, a product sample is one countable or measurable unit of output from the manufacturing process.

Examples of this are one light bulb, one automobile, or one computer mouse. In the case of a bulk product like a soft drink or a batch product like doughnuts, a unit is a specified quantity, often, but not necessarily, equal to the typical unit of sale. It may be a dozen doughnuts or a liter of a soft drink.

Once the purpose of the reliability testing, the sample plan, and the definition of failure are known, then the test method is determined. For manufactured products the idea is to simulate the specified usage conditions as closely as practical. This may require some advance planning. Sometimes test fixtures must be custom-built. Often these are operational mock-ups, like a repeating automatic car-door closer. Sometimes the testing can be done with commercially available equipment. Environmental conditions are often artificially produced with commercially available equipment, like a temperature chamber simulating arctic cold or desert heat.

Like processes, reliability of products is typically measured as simple failure rate (FR), mean time to failure (MTF), or mean time between failures (MTBF). When MTF or MTBF is too low, it indicates the product samples will fail sooner than specified. A high FR also implies that they are more likely to fail or fail more often. In either case, when reliability testing reveals a low MTF or MTBF, or a high FR, then the lot from which the samples were drawn is considered to be nonconforming; that is, the reliability is too low. The lot should be segregated and dispositioned like any other inspection or test failure. Investigation of cause and development of *corrective action* is called for, especially on safety-critical items. If the samples were not production, but

simply developmental builds, then they probably do not
need segregation and disposition, but failure analysis and
corrective action would still be in order to improve the product reliability.

Table 4-1 gives the formulas for calculating FR, MTF,
and MTBF from reliability test results, as well as advice on
their usage.

MTF AND MTBF TESTING

MTF for a product is obtained by running the test and
recording the time from initial test start- up to the first failure. Then record time from start -up to the second failure,
and then the third, and so on. If determining a previously
unknown MTF, continue until all the sample parts fail, then
compute the average time. This is the MTF. If verifying a
specified MTF, then continue until the specified test time or
number of failures is reached.

MTBF is obtained by running the test continuously and
recording the elapsed time between each successive failure,
rather than start-up as with MTF. Then compute the average
elapsed time. When measuring reliability by MTBF, continue until all the sample parts fail, and then compute the average time, whether you are determining an unknown MTBF or
verifying a specified one.

Like FR testing, MTF and MTBF testing are often accelerated. As always, the accelerating factors must be specified
in the test specification and indicated in the test report.

Table 4-1. Formulas For Failure Rate Calculation

Failure Rate Measure	Formula	Usage
FR	$(F/N)Y$	Number of failures (F) divided by sample size (N) multiplied by denomination (Y) 100 for %, 1000 for parts per thousand, or 1,000,000 for parts per million (ppm).
MTF/MTTF	$\Sigma(T_N - T_0)/N$	Measure the elapsed time form start to failure $(T_N - T_0)$ for each sample. Total the elapsed times and divide by sample size N to get mean time to failure.
MTBF (single mode)	$\Sigma(T_N - T_N{-}1)/N$	Measure the elapsed time between one failure and the next failure of the same failure mode $(T_N - T_{N-1})$. Do this for each sample. Total the elapsed times and divide by sample size N to get the mean time between failures.
MTBF (multiple modes)	$\Sigma(T_N - T_{N-1})/N$	Measure the elapsed time between one failure and the next failure regardless of failure mode $(T_N - T_{N-1})$. Do this for each sample. Total the elapsed times and divide by sample size N to get mean time between failures.
Subassembly Failure Rate	$\Sigma(\mathbf{FR_1...FR_x})$	Total the failure rates (due to any component) of the individual components 1 through X where X is the number of components in the subassembly.

FAILURE RATE (FR) TESTING

The failure rate for the product is the number of product samples that do not perform in the specified manner when the test is run. FR testing is also called life testing. It is almost always expressed as the number of failures per 1,000 (or 1,000,000) device operation hours.

If determining an unknown FR, you take the appropriate number of samples and test them to the specified conditions for the appropriate length of time. Transpose the time/sample size as described in Chapter 3, if necessary.

FR testing on purchased items is usually done to verify that the FR is not greater than specified. This is essentially lot conformance testing as applied to reliability. If you are verifying a predicted or specified FR, how long you run the test can be determined by the test results. If the specification is that a certain number of failures will require a specified amount of time, then you continue the test until the specified number of failures is reached and check how much time it took for them to fail. Alternatively, you can run the test until the specified test time is reached and count the number of failures.

Running *accelerated life test* is a deliberate shortening of the time to failure by stressing the test samples beyond normal operating conditions. If the components last a certain time under stress acceleration, this will correspond to a longer operating time under normal conditions. It is a type of time compression for the reliability test. Time to failure is compressed by stressing the samples through increasing a chosen condition or set of conditions. The conditions to accelerate the test are often either the ones most likely to occur during mis-use or abuse, or the one most variable during actual use.

For example, the life testing of a hydraulic valve may be accelerated by higher than normal pressure, or an electric device by higher than normal voltage. High temperature and high humidity are other common accelerating factors. Be careful that the accelerating factor is not itself a failure mode.

When the number of failures at a specific time is too high, or the specified failure quantity occurs too soon, then the lot from which the samples were drawn is considered to have a nonconforming failure rate. If the samples are pro-duction samples, then the lot should be segregated and dis-positioned like any other inspection or test failure.

During product development or improvement, the oper-ating life of a quantity of samples of the same product is often "profiled" by a "bathtub curve." This occurs when the batch or large sample size is tested until every sample unit fails and the number of failures per unit of time is recorded and graphed. For a thousand-hour test, the unit of time might be every twenty-five hours. Initially there will be a high number of failures per unit of time, which gradually decreases. This is known as the *infant mortality period.* Then the number of units of failure per of unit time levels off and remains more or less constant. This is the normal wear-out period. Then the number of failures per unit of time starts to increase again and increases until no more units are left. This is the end-life period. The resulting graph looks like the profile of a bathtub, and hence the name *bathtub curve.* Figure 4-1 illustrates a bathtub curve.

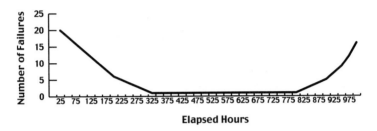

Figure 4-1. The Bathtub Curve

The portion of the graph in Figure 4-1 that decreases steadily to 325 hours is the infant mortality period. 325 to 825 hours mark the normal wear-out period and after 825 hours occurs the end-life period. In testing electronic items, decreasing the slope of the infant mortality section is accomplished by screening out the infant mortality. This is done with a so-called burn-in test. The mechanical equivalent is run-in testing. Burn-in and run-in testing reduce the occurrence of infant mortality, but do not extend the average life of the device.

Reliability is not determined solely on individual component types. Most components, whether electronic or mechanical, are put into subassemblies. These subassemblies all have their own reliabilities, that is, their own failure rates. If the FR of every component in a subassembly is already known, then the subassembly need not be tested to determine the subassembly FR. It can be predicted simply.

Statisticians have long known that for a set of events, all with their own probabilities, the probability of any *one* of either of the events occurring is simply the *sum* of the individual probabilities. The probability of *all* of the events happening at the same time is the *product* of their individual probabilities. For example: you have ten colored balls in a box one red, one blue, and one yellow. The remaining seven are all white. Then the probability of *either* a red *or* a blue *or* a yellow ball being drawn at random on the first three draws is the sum of their probabilities. In this case it is 1/10 + 1/9 +1/8, which is .3361. The probability of getting the red *and* the blue *and* the yellow on the first three tries, is the product of their individual probabilities, 1/10 x 1/9 x 1/8, which is .001388. This is significantly less!

Applied to subassemblies, this means that the FR for subassembly failure due to any *one* of its components failing is the *sum* of their individual FRs. The FR for the subassembly failure due to *all components of a whole group* failing simultaneously, is the *product* of their individual FRs. Such predicting of subassembly failure rates by addition and multiplication applies only to FRs. It does not apply to MTFs and MTBFs.

Example: a simple amplifier circuit consists of one transistor, two resistors, and a capacitor.

Their failures rates are:

transistor FR = 3/ 1,000,000
Resistors FR = 7/1,000,000
Capacitor FR = 2/1,000,000

Then the circuit FR due to any *one* component failing is

000003 + .000007 + .000007 + 000002 = .000019
or 19 out of a million

The failure rate of the transistors is added twice because there are two of them.

However, the FR of the circuit due to failure of all the components in the circuit is

$$.000003 \times .000007 \times .000007 \times .000002 =$$
$$.0000000000000000000252$$

essentially negligible.

Processes and products may even be combined into a system that itself can have a specified goal to be achieved under specified conditions, and therefore defined failure modes. The FR for a system is predicted in the same manner as subassemblies and assemblies. However, the components of a system may include (and are not limited to) processes, manufactured assemblies, materials, people, storage methods, clerical activity, communications, and so on, to name just a few. Each of these has its own FR and must be included in the overall system FR calculation.

System FR is sometimes called mission FR. When this is the case, the success rate is usually expressed rather than the failure rate. Success rate is just 1 − FR. Success rates are also often used for marketing purposes.

CAPABILITY, AVAILABILITY, AND MAINTAINABILITY

The probability of a product performing to a specification is its *product capability*. Just as the FR can also be thought of as the *probability of failure*, the success rate can be thought of as the *probability of success.* Product capability is the probability that a given product will function within the specified tolerance under the specified conditions.

Process capability refers not to the product, but to the process that makes the product. It is estimated by *statistical process control* (SPC). The measures normally used are *Cpk* or *Ppk* for bilateral tolerances and *Cpl* or *Cpu* for unilateral tolerances. When calculated for a given process parameter, it is known as the *capability* index. The capability index is easily translated into a probability of success by multiplying it by three to get a Z value and then looking up the probability on a Z table which can be found in most statistical books and many computer programs. The concept of capability applies not only to products and processes, but also to systems and missions as well.

Since process capability is so easy to calculate by using SPC, one might ask why reliability testing on a process is necessary. The answer lies in the fact that a process capability index calculated by SPC applies to only the one process parameter that was measured, that is, to only one failure mode. So the FR would be for just one cause of failure. You would have to calculate the Cpk for every possible process failure mode and combine their probabilities as done with subassemblies, to predict the overall FR for the entire process. For some processes with 30, 50, or even 100 different failure modes, that would not be practical. Reliability testing for the FR may require less time and effort. Also, some characteristics are not readily measured or specified, so an SPC type capability calculation is not always possible. It is also not practical to calculate product, system, or mission capabilities using SPC for the reasons given above. However, for a very simple process, predicting FR from the Cpk may be a better choice. Remember that Cpk converts to success rate, so to get the failure rate you must convert the Cpk to the success rate and then subtract that from 1.

The *availability* is the probability that the process, product, or system will be available for use as specified. This is simply 1 minus the percentage of downtime, with downtime defined as any time the process, product, or system is not ready for specified use *for any reason*. Another definition of downtime is any time that the process, product, or system cannot be used without the expenditure of additional effort.

Maintainability refers to how easily a process, product, or system in a state of downtime can be made available. This is often measured as the mean time to repair (MTTR), or the mean cost of repair (MCR). To calculate MTTR or MCR, just record the time or cost to repair each failure of each individual sample unit, regardless of failure mode, then compute the average. For a valid MTTR or MCR, be sure to include every sample unit in your calculation.

CHAPTER 5

Interpreting Results

Reliability tests for feasibility are meant to determine if the manufacturing of a product is possible, repeatable, and reproducible to perform as specified. No further interpretation of feasibility testing is valid and no meaning is attached to the results other than whether or not the manufacturing is possible, repeatable, and reproducible. Feasibility testing is usually followed up with further development, design modification, or cancellation.

Reliability verification of outgoing or incoming lots is straightforward. Either the samples meet the specification, or they do not. Nevertheless, it is essential to understand both the limitations of sampling and the true meaning of the test results. Passing reliability verification testing with LTPD- or RQL- type sampling indicates that a particular manufacturer *can* make a product with the required reliability, and for the lot tested, the manufacturer actually *did*. It does not prove the manufacturer always will, nor does it indicate that they usually do. AQL- type sampling on a continuing series of lots would indicate whether they *usually* will, the AQL percent itself being a prediction of how often they *do not*. For example if a continuing series of lots inspected with a 2.5% AQL sample always passes, then the manufacturer *does not* produce the product to the specified reliability an average of 2.5% of the time. This means the manufacturer produces to the reliability specification an average of 97.5% of the time in a continuing series of lots. The confidence you have in this prediction is equal to the confidence level of the sample plan.

Failure rates are usually expressed in terms of number of devices failed per total device operating hours. An FR of 5 parts per 1,000 means that in 1,000 device hours of operation, 5 individual devices failed. Device hours equal the number of devices that are operating times the number of hours they operated. For an electric toggle switch, 1,000 device operation hours may be 1,000 switches operating for 1 hour or 100 switches operating for 10 hours, 10 switches operating for 100 hours, or any combination of devices and hours that multiplies to 1,000. Some devices with low failure rates have their FR expressed in parts per million, but, again, unless otherwise specified, this is number of devices failed per million device hours.

Once the reliability test results are obtained, they are compared to the specification so that one can tell if the reliability is sufficient or not. A reliability better than expected is not a problem from a quality perspective, but may be of interest to sales people or to the customer. Reliabilities not meeting the minimum requirements call for corrective actions. These may be design changes, material changes, maintenance schedule changes, or even a modification of manufacturing or assembly techniques. See Table 5-1 for a summary

Table 5-1. Reliability Test Result Interpretation

Note that reliability results for products and for processes are interpreted the same way.

This Result	Indicates This
Feasibility test is not repeatable but not reproducible	One setup has better equipment or material or one employee or team is doing something different.
Failure rate too high	The probability that the device tested will fail under the specified conditions is too high, thus using the device increases risk to the customer.
MTF less time than specified	There is increased probability that the device will fail sooner than specified. Repair of replacement will have to be made more frequently. There will be more maintenance and downtime with higher cost.
MTF longer time than specified	There is increased probability that the device will operate for a longer time than specified. This may lower warranty costs.
MTBF less time than specified	The device fails more frequently than specified. Repair or replacement will have to be made more frequently. There will be more maintenance and downtime with higher cost.
MTBF longer time than specified	The device will need fewer repairs. There will be less downtime and there may be lower warranty costs.
Sample fails verification test	The proportion of the lot having insufficient reliability is a greater proportion than the AQL; i.e., if a 2.5% AQL sample fails it verification test, then more than 2.5% of the lot has insufficient reliability.

of reliability test result interpretation. Details and further clarification are given below.

MTF and MTBF are both mean times, that is, average times to failure or between failures. Like any average, they are a mathematical construct computed from raw data. The raw data vary around the mean, like any population. But average alone is not the only indicator of central tendency, nor does it tell you about variation.

In normally distributed populations, the average and the mode (most common value) are not significantly different. In perfectly normal distributions, they are equal. The average is also the center point of the distribution range. This is also true of binomial and Poisson distributions. It is not true for exponential distributions or any distribution that is significantly skewed. The more skewed the distribution is, the farther away from the center the mode and the average will be. On exponential distributions, the mode is at the extreme end and the average is about 37% from that end.

Therefore, you cannot interpret MTF or MTBF as being that value in which 50% will fail, nor can you consider it the most common or most probable time of failure. It is simply the mathematically computed average time. For this reason, reliability reports often include a B=.50 value. This is the elapsed time at which 50% of the samples failed. Sometimes B=.10 is also included. Any B = x time is the elapsed time at which x percent failed.

Ideally, in addition to the mean time, a reliability test result should also tell you the standard deviation of the mean so as to tell the amount of variation encountered during the test. This is important because it influences the confidence you can have in the test results and may also indicate how well controlled the manufacturing process and testing practices are. Sometimes a wide variation in what should be a very uniform lot indicates a handling or storage issue.

In the process of reviewing MTBF results, it is also necessary to know if the result is a single failure mode, a prescribed set of failure modes, or any failure mode. You also need to know if repairs were made during the life test and if the sampling is with or without replacement.

Whenever reliability testing is performed during the development phase of the product or process, the results of the reliability testing are most significant. They identify failure modes for the FMEA. This takes the guesswork out of creating the FMEA and gives it a factual basis. When the failure rate is too high, the probability of occurrence portion of the RPN increases. If the failure is major or critical then the severity component of the RPN is high. MTF or MTBF has a similar effect on the RPN. In any case, poor reliability should be properly documented on the FMEA and addressed with corrective action.

CHAPTER 6

IMPROVING RELIABILITY

When reliability test results are not as desired, corrective action is your next step. While the corrective action you take obviously depends on the devices tested, their design and fabrication, and so on. The corrective action also depends on your reasons for performing the test.

If you were testing to determine feasibility, your test failed because the process was either not repeatable or not reproducible. In either case, look for a difference from one process run to the next, and try to determine what was different. Was all the raw material from the exact same lot? Was the operator's technique exactly the same? Were there any differences in the process settings? What about the environment — things like temperature, humidity, and so on? If you cannot eliminate, or at least significantly reduce, your sources of variation then consider redesigning the process or product to make it more robust.

When you perform a reliability verification test on a shipment from a vendor and the reliability is not good enough, corrective action is also warranted. Request corrective action from the vendor, or change vendors. Be sure to provide details of how you tested the device and send samples of failures to the vendor. If you were verifying a production lot of your own, then return samples and give test details of failure to the appropriate people in your organization. Do not forget to update your FMEA once you have an effective corrective action.

If you performed the reliability test to determine the reliability of a new design, then failure analysis is especially important. You need to know exactly why the units failed so you can determine what to change if you want to improve the reliability.

If the failure was that the material cracked, or sheared, or other forms of material failure occurred, then you can either select a different material or change the shape of the broken part to make it more resistant. Typically, material strength should be from two to four times the stress or strain the part will endure in actual use.

If the failure is electronic, failure rates and times to failure can be improved by using components with better reliability rating, though these are more expensive.

Often any failure type, mechanical or electrical/electronic, can be reduced by increasing the energy, that is, heat dissipation during use, Heat sinks, cooling fans, and improved ventilation all help reduce heat. In mechanical motion, heat generation is caused by friction, and so lubrication is critical. A wide variety of lubricants are available with different heat dissipation properties.

GLOSSARY

ACCELERATING FACTOR: A test condition, often environmental, that is set to a value that provides additional stress on the samples, so as to reduce test time by decreasing the amount of time the sample takes to fail.

ACCELERATED LIFE TEST: An operating life test to which one or more accelerating factors have been applied.

ALPHA (α): The risk of rejecting a good part due to sampling, often expressed as a percent. Also called producer's risk.

AVAILABILITY: The percent of time something may be used in its present condition without further unplanned effort or activity.

AVERAGE QUALITY LEVEL (AQL): Characteristics of a sampling plan indicating that average percent of rejects in a continuing series of lots which the sampling plan will allow to pass.

BATHTUB CURVE: A graph of failure rates over time having a characteristic bathtub shape and indicating the rates and times of the infant mortality period, normal wear out period, and end of life period.

BETA (β): The risk of accepting a bad part due to sampling. It is expressed as a percent and often called consumer's risk.

BURN-IN TEST: The reduction or screening out of infant mortality failures by applying power and sometimes stress, then removing or replacing the failure that occurs during the infant mortality period.

Bx: The time or number of operating cycles at which x percent of the test samples failed.

CAPABILITY: The ability of a process or device to operate within the specified tolerance limits. Usually measured as Cpk, Ppk, Cpl, or Cpu.

CENTRAL LIMIT THEOREM: A theorem in statistics according to which when a group of averages is calculated from a group of samples, the averages themselves will be normally distributed regardless of the distribution of the population from which the samples were drawn.

CONFIDENCE LEVEL: The degree of confidence one has in a sample or test result. It is expressed as a probability of not being in error and is equal to 1 minus the total risk. For samples, this is 1 minus (alpha + beta), or $1-(\alpha + \beta)$.

CORRECTIVE ACTION: Action taken to eliminate the root cause of one or more failure modes so as to improve reliability.

Cpk: A measure of process capability applied to characteristics having both upper and lower tolerance limits. It is the lesser of Cpu and Cpl and is often used in statistical process control. It can be converted mathematically into a failure rate prediction.

Cpl: A measure of process capability for characteristics having only the lower tolerance limit, applicable to specifications having no maximum.

Cpu: A measure of processcapability characteristics having only the upper tolerance limit, applicable to specifications having no minimum.

DATA TRANSFORMATION: The normalization of data through applying algebraic formulae to the raw data to effect normal distribution of the data.

DESIGNING ACTIVITY: The person, department, or company having responsibility for the design of a product, or the act of producing the design.

DEVICE-HOUR: A single sample unit of one device operating for one hour.

DEVICE OPERATION CYCLES: The total number of sample units of a device multiplied by the total number of cycles of operation.

DEVICE OPERATION HOURS: The total number of sample units of a device multiplied by the total number of hours they are in operation.

DOUBLE SAMPLING: A sampling scheme in which a small sample is taken and if the number of rejects is less than the reject number, but more than the accept number, then a second sample size is taken on which the accept or reject decision is made.

EXPONENTIAL SAMPLING PLAN: A sampling plan based on the exponential distribution.

FAILURE MODE: The cause of failure or the symptom resulting from a failure.

FAILURE MODE AND EFFECTS ANALYSIS (FMEA): A listing of failure modes, severity of their effects, probability of occurrence, and likelihood of customer rejection. It is used to determine the need for preventive action and to determine the types of control needed. Actions taken and types of control are part of the FMEA report.

FAILURE RATE (FR): The number of failures per 1,000 (or 1,000,000) device-hours. Failure rate can also refer to the probability of failure or the predicted quantity of failures.

FEASIBILITY STUDY: A test or analysis to determine if a proposed product can be made with the proposed process and that the process has repeatability and reproducibly.

FMEA: See Failure Mode and Effects Analysis.

FR: See Failure Rate.

FREQUENCY DISTRIBUTION: The shape of a histogram and/or the corresponding equation having that shape as its graph.

HISTOGRAM: A graph of the frequency of occurrence for each of the various measured or count values of the data or the graph of the number of data values that fall within various ranges of values.

INFANT MORTALITY PERIOD: The period early in the operating time of a device or process in which the failure rate is initially high and decreases steadily before leveling off.

LOT TOLERANCE PERCENT DEFECTIVE (LTPD): A characteristic of rejectable quality level (RQL) sampling plans, it is the maximum percent of rejects a sample plan will accept from an isolated or infrequent lot.

MAINTAINABILITY: The ease or cost effectiveness of maintaining a device or process. Often it is measured in the mean time to repair the device or process or the mean cost of repair.

MEAN COST OF REPAIR (MCR): A measure of maintainability based on repair cost.

MEAN TIME BETWEEN FAILURES (MTBF): The average time between one failure and the next during a reliability test.

MEAN TIME TO FAILURE (MTF or MTTF): The average time to failure of a device calculated from the elapsed time to failure for all the samples in an operating life test.

MEAN TIME TO REPAIR A measure of maintainability based on repair time.

MTBF: See Mean Time Between Failures.

MTF or MTTF: See Mean Time to Failure.

MTTR: See Mean Time To Repair.

MULTIPLE FAILURE MODE: Failure for more than one reason or symptom. This may be applied to a single sample unit failing for more than one failure mode, or a group of sample units that fail for a variety of failure modes, even though only one mode applies to any one sample unit.

MULTIPLE SAMPLING: Similar to double sampling except that the accept or reject decision is based on more than two drawings of samples.

NONSTATISTICAL SAMPLING: Sampling not based on any particular frequency distribution.

NORMAL DISTRIBUTION: The usual bell-shaped distribution so often found in nature.

NORMALIZATION: Making data that is not normally distributed become normally distributed by application of the central limit theorem or a data transformation.

OPERATING LIFE: The average amount of time or number of operations a device or process will function as specified prior to failure. Often measured in hours or operation cycles.

OPERATION CYCLE: One full operation of a process or complete function of a device.

OPERATIONAL PARAMETERS: The specified conditions under which a reliability test is performed. This includes the environmental conditions like temperature and humidity, but also the power input and settings of the device being tested, for example, 120 volts or 200 strokes per minute.

POPULATION: The total number of devices from which a sample is drawn.

Ppk: Same as Cpk but calculated using actual root-mean-square (RMS) standard deviation rather than the R-bar/d2 estimate of variation.

PREVENTIVE ACTION: Action taken prior to production of sample units to prevent one or more failure modes. The need for preventive action is identified by the failure mode and effects analysis.

PROBABILITY OF FAILURE: The number of devices that can be expected to fail expressed as a percent of the total number of devices, or the number of failures expressed as a percent of opportunities for failure.

PROBABILITY OF SUCCESS: The number of devices that do not fail expressed as a percent of the total number of devices or opportunities . Often this is calculated as 1 minus the failure rate.

PROCESS CAPABILITY/RELIABILITY: The ability of a process to produce a product within the specified tolerances.

PRODUCT CAPABILITY/RELIABILITY: The ability of a product to function within the specified tolerances.

REJECTABLE QUALITY LEVEL (RQL): The maxium proportion of defectives in a lot that the sampling plan will allow before rejecting an isolated or infrequent lot.

RELIABILITY: The probability that a process, product, or system will operate as specified, for the specified period of time, under the specified conditions.

REPEATABILITY: The ability of a process to produce results that do not differ significantly from the original result.

REPRODUCIBILITY: The ability of a process or person to reproduce the results of the process or person that it replaces.

RISK PRIORITY NUMBER (RPN): A measure of the risk of a particular failure mode happening as calculated from the combined risks of probability of occurrence, severity of occurrence, and effect on (or notice by) the customer.

RPN: See Risk Priority Number..

RQL: See Rejectable Quality Level.

SAMPLE: A subset of a population on which decisions are based after examination, for example, inspection or testing.

SAMPLIMG RISK: The probability of making the wrong decision based on a sample, either accepting a lot that should have been rejected, or rejecting a lot that should have been accepted.

SHAPE PARAMETER: A characteristic of a Weibull distribution that determines the shape of the distribution.

SINGLE FAILURE MODE: A specific type or cause of failure.

SINGLE SAMPLING: A sampling scheme in which only one group of sample units is drawn from the lot

SKEWED DISTRIBUTION: A frequency distribution or histogram having a mode that is not at the center of the distribution range.

SPC: See Statistical Process Control.

STATISTICAL PROCESS CONTROL: The use of statistics and statistically created control charts to signal when a process needs to be adjusted.

SYSTEM FAILURE: The reliability failure of a combination of products, processes, people, etc.

TEST VALIDITY: The degree to which a reliability test corresponds to actual usage. Also used to refer to the validity of the test data itself

TIME COMPRESSION: The reduction of test time due to the application of an accelerating factor in a test. Sometimes called time acceleration.

TIME INTERVAL:The elapsed time between events.

TIME-QUANTITY TRANSPOSITION: The changing of either time or quantity such that the decrease of one causes an increase in the other.

TIME TO FAILURE: The elapsed time from a reference time to the time of failure. The reference time is usually, but not necessarily, the time the test begins.

WEIBULL DISTRIBUTION: A family of certain types of frequency distributions, the shape of which is determined by a shape parameter. The exact Weibull function, which generates numbers that follow a Weibull distriubtion, is also determined by a scale parameter and a location parameter. While the Weibull function is often used to determine the type of sample plan, it has other uses in calculating probabilities.

ABOUT THE AUTHOR

Ronald Blank has a Bachelor's degree from Southern Connecticut State University and a Doctor of Engineering Degree from Trinity University. His career in quality and reliability spans 25 years in industry and includes reliability engineering in semiconductor manufacturing as well as quality engineering and management in both military avionics and automotive fuel systems. He also has eight years experience teaching advanced statistics and reliability to engineers and other technical personnel. He has been a member of the American Society for Quality for more than 20 years.

OTHER BOOKS IN THE "BASICS" SERIES

The Basics of Benchmarking
Robert Daamelio
80 pp., 1995, Item QRBENCH — $9.95

The Basics of Cross-Functional Teams
Henry J. Lindborg, Ph.D.
80 pp., 1997, Item QRCFT — $9.95

The Basics of FMEA
Robin E. McDermott, Raymond J. Mikulak, and Michael R. Beauregard
80 pp., 1996, Item QFMEA — $9.95

The Basics of Idea Generation
Donna Greiner
80 pp., 1997, Item QRIDEA — $9.95

The Basics of Performance Measurement
Jerry L. Harbour, Ph.D.
80 pp., 1997, QRPM — $9.95

The Basics of Quality Auditing
Ronald Blank
80 pp., 1999, Item QRAUDIT — $9.95

Details are available at www.productivitypress.com